The Micro World of
DUST MITES
AND OTHER MICROSCOPIC
CREATURES

by Melissa Mayer

CAPSTONE PRESS
a capstone imprint

T0050807

Published by Capstone Press, an imprint of Capstone
1710 Roe Crest Drive, North Mankato, Minnesota 56003
capstonepub.com

Library of Congress Cataloging-in-Publication Data is available on the Library of Congress website
ISBN: 9781663976840 (hardcover)
ISBN: 9781666321067 (paperback)
ISBN: 9781666321074 (ebook PDF)

Summary: There are animals all around that people can't see without a microscope. As people shed dead skin cells, thousands of dust mites gobble them up. Tiny creatures called tardigrades can survive in Earth's coldest and hottest places and even in space! Discover amazing, weird, and sometimes gross facts about these and other microscopic creatures.

Editorial Credits
Editor: Arnold Ringstad; Designer: Sarah Taplin; Production Specialists: Joshua Olson and Laura Manthe

Content Consultant
Michael Schultz, Postdoctoral Researcher, University of Alabama at Birmingham

Image Credits
Getty Images: NNehring, 21, Videologia, 12; NASA: Tony Gray and Kevin O'Connell, 15; National Museum of Natural History, inset 23; Science Source: Eye of Science, 10, 13, Sinclair Stammers, 24; Shutterstock: Allexxandar, background 23, Choksawatdikorn, bottom left 5, Craig Lambert Photography, background 5, Elizaveta Galitckaia, 7, F.Neidl, 17, I. Noyan Yilmaz, 29, Juan Gaertner, 9, Lebendkulturen.de, 26, 27, Peter is Shaw 1991, 18, peterschreiber.media, Cover, Petr Smagin, 6

TABLE OF CONTENTS

Words in **bold** are in the glossary.

LIFE AT THE MICRO SCALE

Animals on Earth come in many shapes and sizes. Huge whales swim through the sea. Eagles dive from the sky to catch a meal. Snakes slither across dry deserts. Mosquitoes buzz around people's heads.

People can see all of these animals. But there are many other animals that are much harder to see. They are far smaller. Some of these creatures are **microscopic**. They may be too small to see with just the eyes.

Think about the smallest things you can see. You can probably see a sesame seed. These are about 1 millimeter (mm) long. You might be able to just barely see the width of a human hair, which is around 0.1 mm. Microscopic animals are usually between these two sizes.

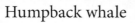

Humpback whale

Large animals are easy to see on land and in the oceans. But many microscopic creatures, such as copepods, also live on Earth.

Copepods seen through a microscope

To see microscopic animals, the human eye needs help. This is especially true if you want to see small details.

A magnifying glass is one way to do this. It uses a single lens to make an object look a bit larger. Another way is to use a **compound microscope**. This tool uses multiple lenses. It may make an object look 1,000 times bigger than normal.

Compound microscope

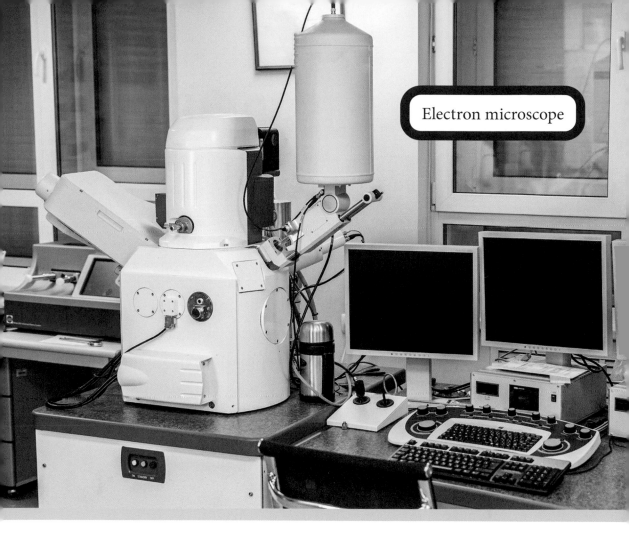

Electron microscope

Scientists use even more powerful microscopes.
These are known as electron microscopes. They
are big and expensive. They can make objects look
50 million times bigger! This is useful for seeing every
tiny detail of a microscopic animal.

MICROSCOPIC CREATURES ON LAND

Dust mites are about 0.5 mm across. They have eight wriggling legs, and they're related to spiders. These mites might live in your bed! Humans are always shedding dead skin. That includes while they sleep. Dust mites gobble it up.

FACT

Dust mites live for 60 to 120 days. Some dust mite **species** poop up to 20 times per day!

Mattresses are a great place to find dead skin. The mites also need to stay moist. Humans provide water with their breath and sweat. One mattress can host millions of mites.

Dust mites crawl along the fibers in a pillow.

Dust mites don't bite or sting. However, some people are **allergic** to them. Mites shed their outer skins. Those skins, along with mite poop, can drift into the air. People can breathe in those substances. People who are allergic may sneeze or cough.

Eyelash mites can be seen in great detail through an electron microscope.

Eyelash mites are even smaller. They can be as small as 0.15 mm. These mites live on the faces of people. They eat oil and skin cells there. The mites like the dark, so they burrow into the openings where eyelashes grow. At night, they climb out and crawl around.

An eyelash mite lives only about two weeks. It can't poop, so its waste builds up inside its body until it dies. Then, all that poop oozes out.

Eyelash mites don't usually bother people. However, too many of them can cause skin problems. But there's good news for kids. Kids have less oil on their faces than adults. Less oil means fewer eyelash mites.

Tardigrades are usually around 0.5 mm long. They have eight short legs. Each leg ends in tiny claws. Tardigrades' mouths are tubes dotted with sharp crystals. Those are handy for poking into plant and animal cells to suck out what's inside.

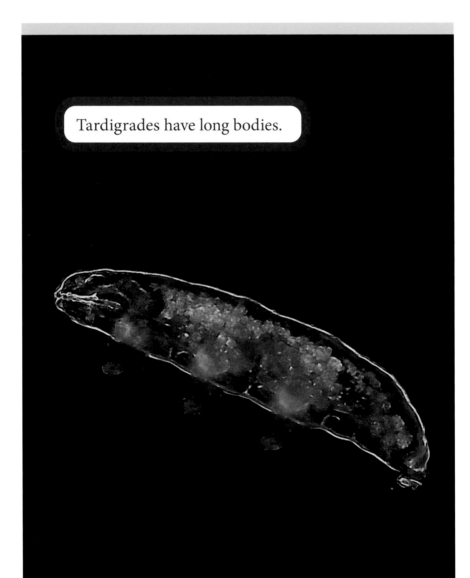

Tardigrades have long bodies.

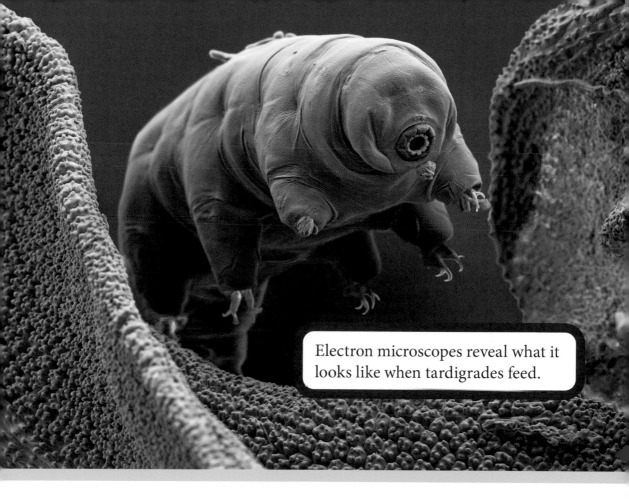

Electron microscopes reveal what it looks like when tardigrades feed.

There are about 1,300 species of tardigrades. They live all over the world. Some are found in deep seas. Others are on tall mountains. They even live in deserts.

Tardigrades need a little bit of water to stay moist. On land, they often spend time in damp moss. That's why some people call them moss piglets. Another nickname for them is water bears.

Tardigrades can survive harsh conditions on land and in the water. They can live through freezing or boiling temperatures. They aren't bothered by the pressure deep in the ocean. Scientists think special proteins protect tardigrade **DNA** when faced with extreme conditions.

Tardigrades have another survival trick. When it's too dry, they push almost all the water out of their bodies. Then they curl into a ball to wait for more moisture to arrive. Scientists call this tun form.

Tardigrades can survive in tun form for decades without food or water. They can even survive in outer space like that. They're the only animal that has ever been unprotected in space and lived.

TARDIGRADES ON THE MOON

In 2019, a spacecraft carrying tardigrades crashed on the moon. It spilled thousands of them. Scientists think they probably survived. But they would need water to become active again.

A June 2021 launch sent tardigrades to the International Space Station. Astronauts studied how these creatures survive extreme conditions.

Nematodes are smooth worms. Some are as small as 0.3 mm. Scientists have named about 20,000 kinds of nematodes. There may be a half million more.

There are tons of nematodes in the soil. A single teaspoon of soil may have more than 100 of them.

Many nematodes are **parasites**. Hookworms are one example. They are human parasites. Hookworm eggs can pass from infected poop into the soil. Then they hatch into microscopic **larvae**. Those larvae can slide through the skin of a bare foot. The infection can cause pain, diarrhea, and tiredness.

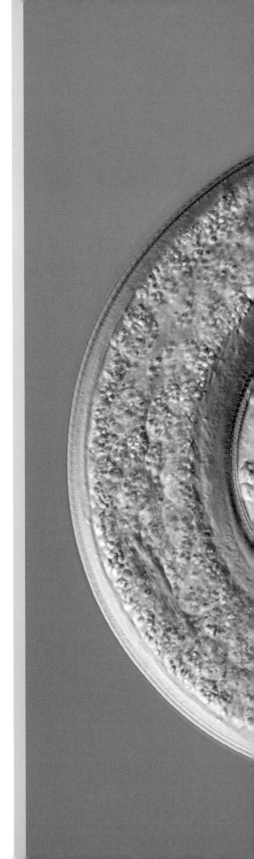

Some nematodes eat tiny pieces of algae in the ocean.

Gardeners can add nematodes to their watering cans and use these creatures to kill garden pests.

Some soil nematodes can be helpful. They are parasites to pests. They may follow a trail of pest poop. Then they crawl inside the pest and kill it. Some people buy these nematodes to kill garden pests naturally.

Scientists study a soil nematode called *C. elegans*. Even though they are tiny, the way these worms develop has some things in common with humans. Studying them can help scientists learn more about how our bodies work.

Astronauts work with *C. elegans* and other helpful nematodes in space. They're learning how these micro creatures survive on the International Space Station.

FACT

In 2003, the space shuttle *Columbia* exploded. Seven astronauts died. Nematodes on board for research were the only survivors of the disaster.

MICROSCOPIC CREATURES IN THE WATER

Rotifers are water animals with antennae and up to five eyes. They measure 0.2 mm to 0.5 mm across. Some swim or inch along the floor of a body of water. Others live in tubes that they create. Still others stick themselves to the floor. Then they wait for food to float by.

Rotifers eat tiny plants and animals in the water. They have a ring of **cilia** near their mouths. The cilia act like fingers. They pull in water. The rotifers sift through the water for food.

FACT

Rotifers called bdelloids are all female. Mother bdelloids copy themselves to make daughters.

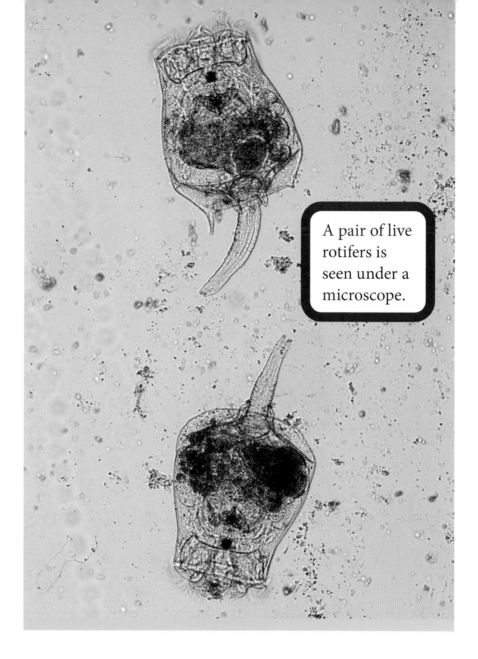

A pair of live rotifers is seen under a microscope.

These animals may live only a few weeks. Some male rotifers don't have digestive systems. They don't live long enough to eat.

Loriciferans are sea animals. They are about 0.1 mm to 0.5 mm in size. Some are so tiny that they live between the grains of sand on the seafloor.

These animals have been around for more than 500 million years. That's even before the time of dinosaurs! Scientists discovered them in the 1970s but didn't name them until 1983.

Loriciferans don't have arms or legs. They have a tube mouth that extends like a telescope. These creatures have a body with a shell. They can pull their mouth and head inside the shell.

LIVING WITHOUT OXYGEN

In 2010, scientists found loriciferans at the bottom of the Mediterranean Sea. The loriciferans there live in very salty mud. There is no oxygen in this area. Scientists are studying these creatures in the seabed.

Many loriciferans have been found off the coast of Florida.

Loriciferan seen through a microscope

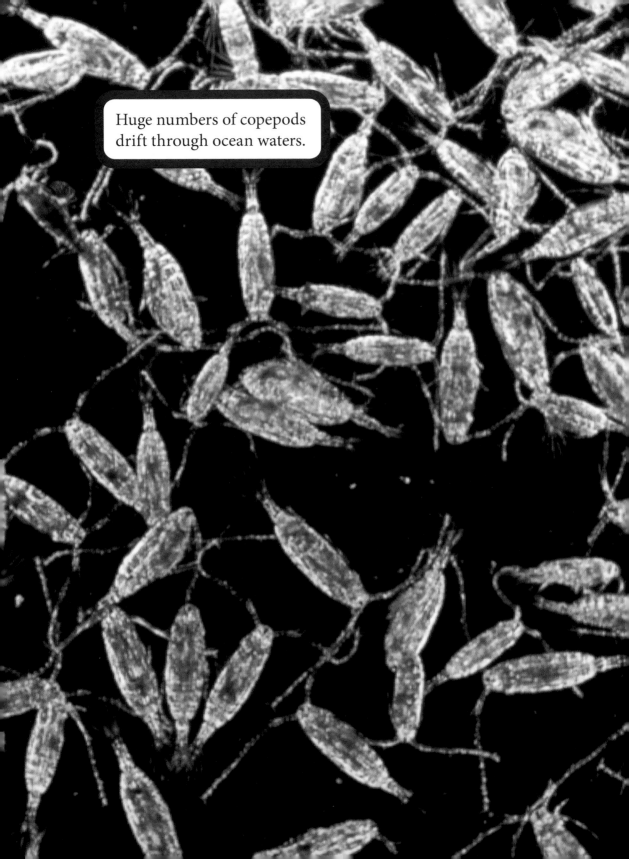

Huge numbers of copepods drift through ocean waters.

Copepods measure from 0.2 mm to 2 mm. They are related to lobsters. These creatures live in every type of water. That includes polar ice water and boiling hot deep-sea vents. You can even find copepods in puddles and in piles of wet leaves!

Copepods are an important part of **plankton** pastures. These are big clouds of tiny plants and animals that float along in the ocean. Bigger animals scoop up mouthfuls of them. Without these food sources, many fish and whales couldn't survive.

Some copepods paddle their antennae and legs like oars. They can reach speeds of 295 feet (90 meters) per hour. That's like a human swimming 50 miles (80 kilometers) per hour!

Water fleas are as small as 0.2 mm across. They are clear with one dark eye. They have a shell and several pairs of legs with hooks. They usually swim in **fresh water** and eat plankton.

Water flea mothers copy themselves to make daughters. Sometimes there isn't enough food to support new water fleas, or the water may be too crowded. But water fleas can still reproduce. They turn a bright copper color. Then they produce a few males to help them lay special eggs.

The scientific name for the most common species of water flea is *Daphnia pulex*.

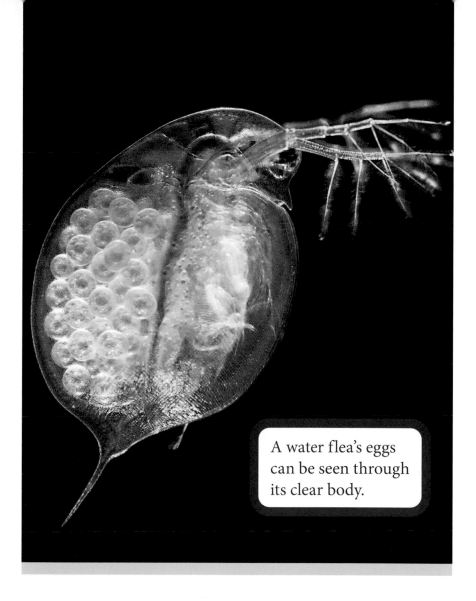

A water flea's eggs can be seen through its clear body.

These eggs are very tough and won't hatch until conditions are good again. Some of them don't hatch for decades or even centuries! Scientists use those eggs like a time capsule to learn about changes in the water over time.

Microscopic creatures might be tiny. But they are a huge part of life on Earth. Many of these animals are near the base of **food webs**. Without them, larger animals couldn't survive.

Microscopic creatures are important to science. Some help scientists answer big questions about the human body. Others have clever ways to survive harsh conditions. Scientists study how these creatures work.

Nobody knows how many species of animals exist. Some scientists think up to 86 percent of species are still unknown. There are tons of creatures out there to discover. New microscopic creatures could be hiding in plain sight!

Scientists collect samples from nature to help learn more about microscopic creatures.

GLOSSARY

allergic (uh-LER-jic)—having a harmful reaction to a substance

cilia (SILL-ee-uh)—tiny hairs used for movement or sensing

compound microscope (com-POUND MY-kruh-skohp)—an instrument with two lenses that makes objects look bigger

DNA (dee-en-A)—short for deoxyribonucleic acid, the molecule inside a living thing that includes instructions for that living thing's traits

food web (FOOD WEB)—a map of how energy passes from the sun to plants to animals through eating

fresh water (FRESH WAW-tur)—water that doesn't have salt in it, usually found in lakes and rivers

larva (LAR-vuh)—the young form of certain kinds of animals

microscopic (my-kruh-SKAH-pik)—too small to see with the unaided human eye

parasite (PAIR-uh-site)—a creature that relies on a host to survive and causes harm to the host

plankton (PLANK-tun)—a tiny creature that can float in water

species (SPEE-sheez)—a group of similar creatures that can reproduce together

READ MORE

McClanahan, Ben. *We Need Plankton.* Lake Elmo, MN: Focus Readers, 2019.

Rajcak, Hélène, and Damien Laverdunt. *Unseen Worlds.* Greenbelt, MD: What on Earth Books, 2019.

Turner, Matt. *Tiny Creepy Crawlers.* Minneapolis: Hungry Tomato, 2017.

INTERNET SITES

American Museum of Natural History: What Is Microbiology?
amnh.org/explore/ology/microbiology

Arizona State University: Ask a Biologist
askabiologist.asu.edu/

National Geographic Kids: Invertebrates
kids.nationalgeographic.com/animals/invertebrates

INDEX

ABOUT THE AUTHOR

Melissa Mayer is a science writer and former science teacher who's currently working on an M.S. in Entomology. She lives on a tiny urban homestead in Portland, Oregon, with her wife, kids, and way too many animals—dogs, cats, rabbits, chickens, and an ever-growing collection of insects. She's the author of five nonfiction books for children and young adults.